# Testimonials

# Hope

"Just when there was no room left in my hurting heart for love, Jesus Christ became very real to me and gave me hope. It was Living Hope that was born on Christmas morn. It was Living Hope that rescued me. Do you know the power of Hope?"
**Lori Boruff**, Speaker, Author, Life Coach
www.embracedbyhope.com

"Years ago, as a single, unemployed mom, panic set in. God used a woman I'd never met who operated a food pantry from her home to set in motion numerous miracles during the four years I was without work. I humbly realized my loving God would always provide. What hope!"
**Mary Aucoin Kaarto** Author, Speaker. www.marykaarto.com
*HELP for the LAID OFF*

# Peace

"In the hustle and bustle of the holidays, it's easy to get caught up in our to-do list and forget the real reason for the season: Jesus. When we focus on Him, He will keep us in perfect peace and fill our hearts with love and joy."
**Andrea Merrell**, Writer, Editor, Speaker.
www.AndreaMerrell.com

"I believe an accurate view of heaven, really anticipating the joy of your future eternity, can fill your spirit with deep peace. Even in the midst of the chaos of our temporal life, we can drink in deep *shalom* setting our eyes on God's abode."
**Anne Elizabeth Denny**, Speaker, Author, Blogger.
www.AnneElizabethDenny.com

"Peace is quietness to the soul, a stillness down deep, where nothing or no one can touch – but Jesus. I tried to find it in many ways, but only opening my heart to a one-on-one relationship with God allowed the peace that passes all understanding to quiet my soul." www.lorihudson.org
**Lori Hudson**, Speaker. www.stainglassministry.com

# Joy

"I consider the Bethlehem stable. What better place for the Lamb of God to be born? Jesus resigned His heavenly post to share my experience of this fallen world, overcome every temptation I will ever face, and apply His perfect performance to my account. I am saturated with joy unspeakable."
**Sandra Lovelace**, Speaker, Writer, Pursuer.
www.SandraAllenLovelace.com

"In the season of twinkling lights and joy, I bask in the awesome provision of my loving Father, who provided a Savior so that I might not perish, but have life everlasting. This is the best present of all!"
**Elizabeth Brickman**, Author
*THIN & BLESSED*

# Love

"I almost canceled Christmas 2009. I had no joy and no hope. My son's addiction had stolen it. As I pondered my decision, the realization of the gift of the Christ Child filled my heart with unspeakable love and grace. It turned out to be one of our best Christmases ever."
**Sharron K. Cosby**, Author, Speaker.
*Praying for Your Addicted Loved One: 90 in 90*

"I always thought I knew what love was. Until I cared for my ailing husband. It was then, when I put his needs before mine, that I found true love. It's felt deepest when sown, not gathered."
**Ellen E. Gee**, Author, Speaker, Blogger.
*My Mother's Song, A Memoir*

## Books by Melissa Kirk

### Nonfiction

### Grace Warrior Devotional Series

Grace Warrior – *Bathed in Mercy, Clothed in Grace*

Grace Warrior – *At the King's Command*

ADVENT – *Celebrate the Coming*

*...watch for more in the Grace Warrior Devotional Series*

# GRACE WARRIOR DEVOTIONAL SERIES

The *Grace Warrior Devotional Series* is designed to enhance the reader's relationship with God. Each book in the series stands alone. As a whole, the books in the series build a foundation for kingdom living.

*ADVENT – Celebrate the Coming* encourages the reader to focus on scriptural anticipation. This book can be read during Advent or anytime during the year when a new beginning is experienced or expected.

It begins with a short introduction. From there, it focuses on the topics: Hope, Peace, Joy, and Love. There are seven sections per subject. Worship reading is first and opens a conversation with God about the topic. The next six readings look at the theme from the perspectives of *The Past, The Present, The Future, God's Plan, God's Gift,* and *To Share.*

Each reading is short to encourage time for personal interaction with God through his word and prayer. Although numbered for a four-week journey, the reader should dwell on each topic as long as they wish. There is a discussion guide included for those who would like to read and discuss the devotional together.

# ADVENT

## *Celebrate the Coming*

Grace Warrior Devotional Series

# Melissa Kirk

Grace Warrior

ADVENT – *Celebrate the Coming*

Published by Charlene Publishing
Copyright ©2015 by Melissa Kirk
Cover Design by oberkromdesign.prosite.com.

Scripture quotations are taken from the Holy Bible, New Living Translation, copyright ©1996, 2004, 2007, 2013 by Tyndale House Foundation. Used by permission of Tyndale House Publishers, Inc., Carol Stream, Illinois 60188. All rights reserved.

ISBN-13: 978-0996923101 (Charlene Publishing)
ISBN-10: 0996923101

Published in the United States

First Edition.

To Larry,
my loving husband.

♥

Thank you for encouraging me.
I love you.

# ADVENT – *Celebrate the Coming*
## Contents

## Excerpts

Be sure to meet the woman, GRACE WARRIOR. You can see her and see how her positions change on the covers of the other books in the Grace Warrior Devotional Series

GRACE WARRIOR

Definition:

A child of God, who handles Kingdom business with dignity
and determination.

*"Come, Lord Jesus"*

# Advent

I love Christmas! But, in years past, the chaotic, commercialized, celebration of Christmas sucked the life out of me.

There's the *Final Sales Event of the Season* that happens every weekend. Charity drives, company socials, family dinners, parades, church plays, and band concerts fill the calendar. Apparently, sleep isn't necessary the last six weeks of the year.

Christmas decorations crowding out pumpkins before

the first leaf falls bugs me. Happy Holidays versus Merry Christmas debates on social media are annoying. One Christmas carol per sixty Santa Baby songs on the radio bothers me. And, the Babe-in-a-manger piece haphazardly stuffed between a Ninja Turtle Cowabunga Christmas plaque and a snow globe with Frosty in beachwear sends me over the edge.

For years, I lit up the entire house with twinkling lights. Bah humbug putting that mess away. Once, I did the reverse and simplified. No one appreciated the oranges, apples, and walnuts in their stocking.

My strategies weren't working, but with three children, eleven grandchildren, and a great-grandchild, a full retreat wasn't an option. So, I had a conversation with God after the last yuletide, and through a summer of reflection, I realized the problem. I was misinterpreting the season's rules of engagement. Until now, my battle cry was:

*It's Christmas. I will survive.*

*I will decorate my home fashionably. It's Christmas.*

*I will prepare a large family meal. It's Christmas.*

*I will buy lots of presents. It's Christmas.*

*I will insist everyone experience peace and goodwill or else!*

*It's Christmas. I will survive.*

I had it wrong, and my life was void of all that the Advent season celebrated: hope, peace, joy, and love.

God reminded me that the world's idea of celebration contradicts his, but it's *his* battle, not mine.

He reiterated that Christmas doesn't stop people from hurting. It doesn't take away restlessness or discouragement or loneliness. Hope, peace, joy and love so desperately sought after is found in Christ alone; not in the celebration.

He requested I recall my rank. You may have noticed a whole lot of *I's* in the above thoughts. He did too. God wants my participation in his kingdom affairs, *under* his authority.

So, you'll still find me in the midst of the chaotic, commercialized, celebration of Christmas, but hopefully a new me; with a clearer understanding of God's seasonal rules of engagement. My duty as a grace warrior for the kingdom is to follow his simple directives: converse and share.

When my hands dig through the sixty percent off pile of pajamas, hope can be shared by buying a set for the children's shelter and praying for the child who wears them. While waiting in line behind the young couple who is trying to decide if they can afford the milk, diapers, *and* discounted plastic toy truck, peace can be shared by slipping a ten dollar bill their way and inviting them to the free church community meal. Joy can be shared by reciting a few lines from *The Magnificat* with a new mother. As the community parade floats pass by, love can be shared by telling the person standing next to me about God's faithfulness. Here's my new battle cry.

*God sent his Son, Jesus. He is coming again, soon.*

*God sent a star to light our way. Celebrate and share hope.*

*God's heavenly hosts cried out. Celebrate and share peace.*

*God's gift is eternal life. Celebrate and share joy.*

*God's gift is available to all. Celebrate and share love.*

*God sent his Son, Jesus. He is coming again, soon.*

Whether your Advent season is packed with festivities, or mostly alone time, God's directives are the same: converse and share.

The gifts people want are your time, your smile, your touch, and most importantly, your testimony of the celebration *you* have because you received God's gift of eternal life; free from death and decay.

If you haven't accepted his gift, my prayer is that you'll have a personal conversation with the Almighty. It's because of his Son; we celebrate the Advent season.

# HOPE

*Definition: anticipating a desired conclusion*

"If it were not for hopes, the heart would break."

Thomas Fuller

# Day 1 - HOPE

# In Worship

**Proclamation**

**Hope**

Hope is a gift from God, *the Father*, made possible through Jesus, *God's Son*. I accept the gift through faith in the victory over death by Jesus, *my Lord*.

**What do I hope for?**

I wait eagerly for my priceless inheritance. God promises me an estate, free from strife and discord. God promises me a new body, free from death and decay.

**Where is the foundation of my hope?**

In the Lord. Read *Psalm 39:7*.

**Who assures my hope?**

The Holy Spirit. Read *II Corinthians 5:4-5*.

**Receiving God's Word**

"All praise to God, the Father of our Lord Jesus Christ. It is by his great mercy that we have been born again, because God raised Jesus Christ from the dead. Now we live with great expectation, and we have a priceless inheritance—an inheritance that is kept in heaven for you, pure and undefiled, beyond the reach of change and decay."

*I Peter 1:3-4*

**Connecting with God's Word**

What is your expectation for the future?

**Responding to God's Word**

Do you have something you want to say to God about hope?

**Celebrate**

What gift from God can you celebrate today?

# Day 2 - HOPE

## The Past

Zechariah, a Jewish priest, was invited to the party. It was a celebration with an abundance of gifts. To name a few:

• God considered Zechariah righteous.

• The priest was chosen to perform the sacred duties in the Holy Place.

• A heavenly being appeared to him.

• God answered his prayer. His wife, Elizabeth, would give him a son.

• The angel, Gabriel, promised the priest joy in his future.

• He learned his son would be obedient to God.

What a celebration! Unfortunately, Zechariah had a problem that interfered with the festivities. Doubt. He was old, and his wife was past childbearing years. Read *Luke 1*.

It's discouraging that many of God's children are like Zechariah. They miss the blessings of the moment because of the grief in their past. It's heart-wrenching that many others haven't accepted the invitation to be part of the family of God.

### Receiving God's Word

"Zechariah said to the angel, 'How can I be sure this will happen? I'm an old man now, and my wife is also well along in years.' Then the angel said, 'I am Gabriel! I stand in the very presence of God. It was he who sent me to bring you this good news! But now, since you didn't believe what I said, you will be silent and unable to speak until the child is born. For my words will certainly be fulfilled at the proper time.'"

*Luke 1:18-20*

### Connecting with God's Word

Is your past interfering with today's blessings? How?

### Responding to God's Word

Is there anything you want to say to God?

### Celebrate

What gift from God can you celebrate today?

# Day 3 - HOPE

## The Present

Driving home from North Carolina, I was exhausted, but optimistic about getting home on time after the long, nine-hour drive. Home was only three more hours away. It'd be dark before I arrived, but familiar roads were just past Memphis, which was only *one* hour away.

Wet drops hit the windshield. I raised the sun visor to discover the sun slipping behind gloomy clouds. The sprinkling escalated to a downpour and the dark clouds blackened. The only glimpses of the road then were when lightning struck too close for comfort.

Gripping the steering wheel tighter, I slowed to a crawl. Thoughts of semi-trucks plowing over me clouded my ability to think. I jerked into the next lane to avoid rear-ending another frightened traveler going slower than me.

Just as panic set in, a small flicker of light appeared in the distance. I followed the light, veering off at the next exit and crossing the overpass.

A lone service station's lights illuminated the entire hill. I parked under the gas pump awning and drew a breath of relief.

The reprieve lasted only a few minutes. Other travelers crowded in for cover, and I reluctantly gave up my spot to those needing fuel.

My phone's weather application showed the location as a pinpoint green spot surrounded by yellow and red. But, I really wanted to get to familiar territory before nightfall, so hoping the storm would dissipate, I headed out again.

Six exits and two near accidents later, reality set in. I exited off and found a hotel for the night. The bright lights over the service desk and a nice gentleman with a sympathetic smile greeted me. I was safe.

My trip didn't go as planned. The unexpected storm encompassed me with dangerous obstacles. Night came too fast. Like the pickup that I passed on the side of the road with emergency blinkers flashing, I succumbed to the elements. Just like the spinning sports car in the middle of the highway had. Like the semi-trucks forging forward, I was headed for destruction. Until I saw the light.

While the tempest still raged outside, I was now safely tucked in waiting for the storm to pass and morning to break. I worried about the pickup, and the vehicle spinning out of control. Did those travelers find refuge?

I'm thankful the light showed me the way. I wished that when I first saw it, I hadn't refused its safety.

**Receiving God's Word**

"And the judgment is based on this fact: God's light came into the world, but people loved the darkness more than the light, for their actions were evil."

*John 3:19*

**Connecting with God's Word**

How do you feel when darkness sets in? Do you find yourself there often?

**Responding to God's Word**

Is there anything you want to say to God?

**Celebrate**

What gift from God can you celebrate today?

# Day 4 - HOPE

# The Future

God says we all live in disobedience. He describes it as a darkness that must be judged.

Because He loves us, God sent his Son, Jesus, to be the light of the world, free to anyone who would accept it.

"The people who walk in darkness will see a great light. For those who live in a land of deep darkness, a light will shine."

*Isaiah 9:2*

The prophet Isaiah described this light as a child that would be born in the future. Read *Isaiah 9:2-7.*

The apostle John described a child of light born several years earlier. Read *John 1:1-5.*

The light that Isaiah and John spoke of was the same. Jesus. He is the hope. He is the everlasting light of the world.

~A simple thought~

You choose to walk either in darkness or in light.

**Receiving God's Word**

"Jesus spoke to the people once more and said, 'I am the light of the world. If you follow me, you won't have to walk in darkness, because you will have the light that leads to life.'"

*John 8:12*

**Connecting with God's Word**

What hope does Jesus give?

**Responding to God's Word**

Is there anything you want to say to God?

**Celebrate**

What gift from God can you celebrate today?

15

# Day 5 - HOPE

# God's Plan

**Receiving God's Word**

**Do you need God's plan?** "For everyone has sinned; we all fall short of God's glorious standard."

*Romans 3: 23*

**Why do you need God's plan?** "For the wages of sin is death, but the free gift of God is eternal life through Christ Jesus our Lord."

*Romans 6:23*

**What is God's plan?** "But God showed his great love for us by sending Christ to die for us while we were still sinners."

*Romans 5:8*

**What is my part in God's plan?** "If you openly declare that Jesus is Lord and believe in your heart that God raised him from the dead, you will be saved. For it is by believing in your heart that you are made right with God, and it is by openly declaring your faith that you are saved."

*Romans 10:9-10*

**Will God's plan work for me?** "For everyone who calls on the name of the LORD will be saved."

*Romans 10:13*

**How can I know God's plan worked for me?** "And I am convinced that nothing can ever separate us from God's love. Neither death nor life, neither angels nor demons, neither our fears for today nor our worries about tomorrow—not even the powers of hell can separate us from God's love."

*Roman 8: 38*

### Connecting with God's Word

Have you accepted God's plan to walk in light?

### Responding to God's Word

Is there anything you want to say to God?

### Celebrate

What gift from God can you celebrate today?

# Day 6 - HOPE

## God's Gift

**Hope changes how God sees us.** The Bible says God calls us his children. We become his heir. Read *1 John 3:1.*

**Hope changes God's focus.** The Bible assures us that the Lord watches over those who place their hope in him. Read *Psalm 33:13-22.*

**Hope changes how we see ourselves.** We join other Christ-Followers, acknowledging we are just travelers passing through the short existence of life and death on this earth, headed to an eternal life in heaven. Read *Hebrews 11:13-16.*

**Hope changes our daily lives.** We are filled with joy, peace, strength, and courage. Read *Romans 15:13* and *Psalm 31:24.*

### Receiving God's Word

"Dear friends, we are already God's children, but he has not yet shown us what we will be like when Christ appears. But we do know that we will be like him, for we will see him as he really is. And all who have this eager expectation will keep themselves pure, just as he is pure."

*I John 3:2-3*

### Connecting with God's Word

How is God's hope different than the world's view of hope?

### Responding to God's Word

Is there anything you want to say to God?

### Celebrate

What gift from God can you celebrate today?

# Day 7 - HOPE

# To Share

To find the new King of the Jews, wise men from distance lands followed an unusual star. When questioned about their journey, they shared the message of hope recorded by one of God's prophets many years earlier. The news disturbed some, but the travelers were joyful.

The influential, wealthy men found the promised Messiah in humble settings. Bowing, they worshiped and showered him with gifts. Read *Matthew 2:1-11*.

We are different than the wise men in that we don't have to travel to meet the King. He meets us where we are. Read *James 4:8*.

In another way, we are just like them. People around us need answers.

Somewhere near you a woman is grieving. A man is stumbling. A teenager is confused. There's a homeless veteran, a sick father, and a worried mother.

They're searching for hope. If you have received the gift of hope, will you share?

### Receiving God's Word

"Instead, you must worship Christ as Lord of your life. And if someone asks about your hope as a believer, always be ready to explain it."

*I Peter 3:15*

### Connecting with God's Word

How can a Christ-Follower explain hope?

### Responding to God's Word

Is there anything you want to say to God?

### Celebrate

What gift from God can you celebrate today?

*Melissa Kirk*

*Dear Lord,*

*Thank you for the hope of everlasting life, free from strife and discord, and death and decay. Thank you for the light of your Son, Jesus. Now, I ask you to fill me with your peace.*

*Amen*

*Melissa Kirk*

# PEACE

*Definition: agreeing to be in harmony*

"There cannot be any peace where there is uncertainty."

D. L. Moody

# Day 1 - PEACE

# In Worship

**Proclamation**

**Peace**

Peace is a gift from God, *the Father*, made possible through Jesus, *God's Son*. I accept the gift through faith in the victory over death by Jesus, *the Prince of Peace*.

**What can I have peace about?**

I trust God's peace to guard my heart and mind about everything. He promises peace beyond anything I can comprehend.

**Who made peace with God possible?**

Jesus Christ. Read *Romans 5:1*.

**Who assists us in accepting peace?**

The Holy Spirit. Read *John 14:27*.

### Receiving God's Word

"But when the Father sends the Advocate as my representative—that is, the Holy Spirit—he will teach you everything and will remind you of everything I have told you. 'I am leaving you with a gift—peace of mind and heart. And the peace I give is a gift the world cannot give. So don't be troubled or afraid.'"

*John 14:26-27*

### Connecting with God's Word

How difficult is it for you to have peace?

### Responding to God's Word

Is there anything you want to say to God about peace?

### Celebrate

What gift from God can you celebrate today?

# Day 2 - PEACE

## The Past

Simeon was invited to the party. There was still an abundance of gifts at the celebration. To name a few:

- The elderly man was considered righteous.
- The Holy Spirit was upon him.
- God promised Simeon he would see the Messiah.
- He held the baby Jesus in his arms.
- He knew he would die in peace.
- He was privileged to bless Jesus' parents.

What a celebration! Nothing got in the way of Simeon's party! Although he had grown old, he still eagerly waited for the promised Messiah, who would rescue him. God answered his prayer. He saw God, *the Son*, in living flesh. Read *Luke 2:25-35*.

It's encouraging to witness the steadfastness of Christ-Followers who intently search out the God's promises in their lives, not willing to miss any blessings.

It's exciting to know everyone has the same opportunity to experience God's peace.

### Receiving God's Word

"Simeon was there. He took the child in his arms and praised God, saying, 'Sovereign Lord, now let your servant die in peace, as you have promised. I have seen your salvation, which you have prepared for all people. He is a light to reveal God to the nations, and he is the glory of your people Israel!'"

*Luke 2:28-32*

### Connecting with God's Word

Do you feel peace while remembering God's promises?

### Responding to God's Word

Is there anything you want to say to God?

### Celebrate

What gift from God can you celebrate today?

# Day 3 - PEACE

## The Present

"Daddy, I'm scared."

The father pulled the tiny balled-up fists from the child's eyes and wrapped his strong hands around them. "I'm right here. Tell me why you're frightened."

"I don't know what's going to happen."

"It's going to be fine. I promise."

"But, how do you know?"

"I know because I've already been there. Rest now."

~

Our family knows how the child felt. Four years ago, my grandson, Gage, was diagnosed with leukemia. The discovery came fast. In just a few days, Gage went from not feeling well to a trip to the local hospital emergency room.

From there, to Arkansas Children's Hospital, Little Rock, AR, and finally to St. Jude Children Research Hospital, Memphis, TN.

Those early days were filled with fear and confusion. I remember my daughter, Melanie, walking into the waiting room at the Little Rock Hospital.

"I can't do this," she cried out.

That's how we all felt. We didn't know what the next day would bring. The doctors and nurses were calm and professional. They assured us Gage would receive the best possible care, but the many questions and unknowns were unsettling.

Soon, a treatment plan started coming together, and although no one offered a guarantee, an unexplainable peace settled over us as we decided to go with the advice of the doctors. In the midst of the crisis, agreeing to focus on the recommendations brought stillness and order.

Six weeks later, Gage was in already in remission and home from the hospital. It was the Thanksgiving holiday.

Holding to tradition, one of the grandchildren was to read a scripture verse for the evening meal prayer. It was Gage's turn.

He didn't just read. He *sang* from Psalm 100! "…Acknowledge that the Lord is God! He made us, and we are his people, the sheep of his pasture. … Give thanks to him and praise his name. For the Lord is good. His unfailing love continues forever, and his faithfulness continues to each generation."

As the Psalm states, we are his people, the sheep of his

pasture. We don't know what comes next, but the Shepherd does. Acknowledging his leadership brings perfect peace.

**Receiving God's Word**

"Then Jesus said, 'Come tc me, all of you who are weary and carry heavy burdens, and I will give you rest. Take my yoke upon you. Let me teach you, because I am humble and gentle at heart, and you will find rest for your souls.'"

*Matthew 11:28-29*

**Connecting with God's Word**

How do you feel when troubles come? Do you rest?

**Responding to God's Word**

Is there anything you want to say to God?

**Celebrate**

What gift from God can you celebrate today?

# Day 4 - PEACE
## The Future

We will experience trouble and feelings of powerlessness in our lives. However, if we trust God, he promises to lift the heaviness and empower us for the future.

"But those who trust in the Lord will find new strength. They will soar high on wings like eagles. They will run and not grow weary. They will walk and not faint."

*Isaiah 40:31*

The prophet Isaiah wrote that even the strongest man will be weak at times. Read *Isaiah 40:30.*

The disciple Matthew wrote that anyone can find rest. Read *Matthew 11:28-30.*

Trusting God is the first step to peace. He is the King, and Jesus is the Prince of Peace.

~A simple thought~

Everyone has a unique comfort level.

### Receiving God's Word

"I have told you all this so that you may have peace in me. Here on earth you will have many trials and sorrows. But take heart, because I have overcome the world."

*John 16:33*

### Connecting with God's Word

Why does Jesus say you can have peace in him?

### Responding to God's Word

Is there anything you want to say to God?

### Celebrate

What gift from God can you celebrate today?

# Day 5 - PEACE

## God's Plan

### Receiving God's Word

**Do you need God's plan?** "Those who love your instructions have great peace and do not stumble."

*Psalm 119:165*

**Why do you need God's plan?** "So letting your sinful nature control your mind leads to death. But letting the Spirit control your mind leads to life and peace."

*Romans 8:6*

**What is God's plan?** "God blesses those who work for peace, for they will be called the children of God."

*Matthew 5:9*

**What is my part in God's plan?** "And let the peace that comes from Christ rule in your hearts. For as members of one body you are called to live in peace. And always be thankful."

*Colossians 3:15*

**Will God's plan work for me?** "And Jesus said to the woman, "Your faith has saved you; go in peace.""

*Luke 7:50*

**How can I know God's plan worked for me?** "And this righteousness will bring peace. Yes, it will bring quietness and confidence forever."

*Isaiah 32:17*

**Connecting with God's Word**

Have you accepted God's peace in your life?

**Responding to God's Word**

Is there anything you want to say to God?

**Celebrate**

What gift from God can you celebrate today?

37

# Day 6 - PEACE

# God's Gift

**Peace changes how God sees us.** The Bible says God calls us his friend when we accept life through his Son, Jesus. We are no longer his enemy. Read *John 15:15.*

**Peace changes God's focus.** The Bible assures us that God will help those who are on his side. Read *Psalm 124.*

**Peace changes how we see ourselves.** We are privileged to stand confident, waiting for God to be worshiped by all. Read *Romans 5:1-2.*

**Peace changes our daily lives.** We see problems differently because we know God is in charge. Read *Romans 5:3-5.*

## Receiving God's Word

"Thou will keep in perfect peace all who trust in you, all whose thoughts are fixed on you."

*Isaiah 26:3*

## Connecting with God's Word

How is God's peace different than the world's view of peace?

## Responding to God's Word

Is there anything you want to say to God?

## Celebrate

What gift from God can you celebrate today?

# Day 7 - PEACE

## To Share

One night, while shepherds took care of the flock, an angel appeared. They were afraid until the angel announced the birth of the Messiah. Heavenly hosts spoke out, "…peace on earth…"

The herdsmen hurried to find the baby, and when they did, their fear turned to insuppressible joy. They shared the news with everyone.

God's message was clear. Salvation had come and was available to all, even to the lowest on the social ladder. Read *Luke 2:8-20.*

We are like the shepherds because we need the peace God offers to all, regardless of our status. We are also like the shepherds because we have an incredible story to tell.

Someone near you feels too unworthy to enter a relationship with God. Distressed, they are searching for peace. There are also people around you who have everything the world offers but are still tormented.

If you have received the gift of peace, will you share?

### Receiving God's Word

"But the wisdom from above is first of all pure. It is also peace loving, gentle at all times, and willing to yield to others. It is full of mercy and the fruit of good deeds. It shows no favoritism and is always sincere. And those who are peacemakers will plant seeds of peace and reap a harvest of righteousness."

*James 3:17-18*

### Connecting with God's Word

How does a Christ-Follower spread peace?

### Responding to God's Word

Is there anything you want to say to God?

### Celebrate

What gift from God can you celebrate today?

*Dear Lord,*

*Thank you for your instructions that lead to peace of mind, heart, and soul. Thank you for sending your Son, Jesus, the Prince of Peace. Now I ask you to fill me with your joy. Amen*

*Melissa Kirk*

# JOY

*Definition: state of contentment*

"The very nature of joy makes nonsense of our common distinction between having and wanting."

C. S. Lewis

# Day 1 - JOY

# In Worship

**Proclamation**

**Joy**

Joy is a gift from God, *the Father*, made possible through Jesus, *God's Son*. I accept the gift through faith in the victory over death by Jesus, *my Deliverer*.

**What can I have joy about?**

Joy is mine because I have trusted God to save me. God is with me. He is my provider. He is my strength. He is my hiding place.

**Who made joy with God possible?**

Jesus. Read *John 15:9-12*.

**Who gives the assurance of joy?**

The Lord. Read *Psalm 34:8-10*.

### Receiving God's Word

"In that day you will sing: 'I will praise you, O Lord! You were angry with me, but not anymore. Now you comfort me. See, God has come to save me. I will trust in him and not be afraid. The Lord God is my strength and my song; he has given me victory.' With joy you will drink deeply from the fountain of salvation!"

*Isaiah 12:1-3*

### Connecting with God's Word

What is the scripture saying to you about your future?

### Responding to God's Word

Is there anything you want to say to God about joy?

### Celebrate

What gift from God can you celebrate today?

# Day 2 - JOY

# The Past

Elizabeth was invited to the party, too. Gifts were everywhere! To name a few:

· God called the elderly woman righteous.

· Elizabeth's desire to have a child was granted.

· She was filled with the Holy Spirit.

· During her own pregnancy, Zechariah's wife was able to assist the mother of Jesus, and listen to the young mother sing praises to the Lord.

· She shared God's instructions when her husband was unable to speak.

· Her son would introduce Jesus as the Messiah.

Elizabeth was one of the first to know the details of the upcoming party and she excitedly participated. Read *Luke 1:23-80.*

How inspiring to witness a mature believer joyfully mentor a younger one. Knowing about God's faithfulness is one thing, but *experiencing* it builds contentment. Elizabeth's joyful response to God's plan at work in their lives brought assurance to Mary.

### Receiving God's Word

"Elizabeth gave a glad cry and exclaimed to Mary, 'God has blessed you above all women, and your child is blessed. Why am I so honored, that the mother of my Lord should visit me? When I heard your greeting, the baby in my womb jumped for joy. You are blessed because you believed that the Lord would do what he said.'"

*Luke 1:42-45*

### Connecting with God's Word

How to you respond when you recognize God's work in someone's life? Do you encourage them?

### Responding to God's Word

Is there anything you want to say to God?

### Celebrate

What gift from God can you celebrate today?

# Day 3 - JOY

# The Present

Grandma Murphy gave me joy.

When I was young, my grandparents were a full day's drive away, so we didn't get to visit often.

I remember climbing out of the car after the long trip and greeting the stocky woman with a twisted gray bun. She was usually outside watering a grassy patch in the yard. What astounded me was her solid footing in bare feet while bees swarmed around her legs. She didn't flinch.

We'd always enter the house through the back. The wood framed screen door would squeak loudly in complaint as it stretched back. Once everyone was inside, the door was released, and with a loud pop, it sealed us inside.

While we were there, it seemed like everything Grandma needed was outside. I'd watch her go in and out that door, every *pop* reassuring me I was safe, away from the bees.

Grandma had a beautiful rose covered bowl that I cherished. She served warm potato salad in it, which I *didn't* love, but always ate, because it was in that beautiful vessel.

I'd hold my breath while the dishes were being

washed. Afraid the fragile bowl might slip from her hands, I'd cringe while Grandma masterfully twirled it around in her sudsy fingers.

She masterfully handled Grandpa, too. I remember one time when his hearing was failing, he kept insisting that Grandma call a distant relative to come over to visit while we were there. Several times, she patiently responded that they were out of town. He wasn't hearing her, though, and persisted.

Finally, without blinking an eye, she picked up the old rotary phone and dialed. After a minute, she put the receiver back in its cradle.

"No answer Jess," she said.

I was sitting close enough to see that the call was never made. She held the connector button down the entire time. The call didn't connect, but Grandpa was content after that.

Memories of her fearless encounters with the bees, controlling the screen door, handling the fragile bowl, and consoling my grandpa were joyful times for me. Not because they were earth shaking events. There were no firecrackers, claps, or admiring crowds.

They were joyful because I was very content watching her at work and taking charge of every situation with ease.

It's the same way with our Father in heaven. The joy he gives is a contentment knowing that he has everything under control.

He can handle the stings, opening and closing of doors, and life's most fragile moments. And yes, he will even occasionally pacify us to settle things down.

Pure joy. It doesn't come like a marching parade. It shows up in the smallest ways to remind us that God is in complete control.

## Receiving God's Word

"But let all who take refuge in you rejoice; let them sing joyful praises forever. Spread your protection over them, that all who love your name may be filled with joy. For you bless the godly, O Lord; you surround them with your shield of love."

*Psalm 5:11-12*

## Connecting with God's Word

What does it feel like knowing that God offers protection?

## Responding to God's Word

Is there anything you want to say to God?

## Celebrate

What gift from God can you celebrate today?

# Day 4 - JOY

# The Future

The Bible says we can deal with anything that comes our way. Jesus set the example for us by enduring the cross. He was able to do so by focusing on joy.

"We do this by keeping our eyes on Jesus, the champion who initiates and perfects our faith. Because of the joy awaiting him, he endured the cross, disregarding its shame. Now he is seated in the place of honor beside God's throne."

*Hebrews 12:1-2*

The psalmist wrote that the heavens, earth, and everything in them would shout for joy because of the justness of God. Read *Psalm 96:11-13*.

David wrote that even every king on earth would recognize the joy of the Lord's ways. Read *Psalm 138:5*.

~A simple thought~

Joy is a fruit of the Holy Spirit who lives in God's children.

### Receiving God's Word

"I have seen you in your sanctuary and gazed upon your power and glory. Your unfailing love is better than life itself; how I praise you! I will praise you as long as I live, lifting up my hands to you in prayer. You satisfy me more than the richest feast. I will praise you with songs of joy."

*Psalm 63:2-5*

### Connecting with God's Word

Why are we satisfied?

### Responding to God's Word

Is there anything you want to say to God?

### Celebrate

What gift from God can you celebrate today?

# Day 5 - JOY

## God's Plan

### Receiving God's Word

**Do you need God's plan?** "The hopes of the godly result in happiness, but the expectations of the wicked come to nothing."

*Proverbs 10:28*

**Why do you need God's plan?** "For the Kingdom of God is not a matter of what we eat or drink, but of living a life of goodness and peace and joy in the Holy Spirit."

*Romans 14:17*

**What is God's plan?** "I pray that God, the source of hope, will fill you completely with joy and peace because you trust in him. Then you will overflow with confident hope through the power of the Holy Spirit."

*Romans 15:13*

**What is my part in God's plan?** "You haven't done this before. Ask, using my name, and you will receive, and you will have abundant joy."

*John 16:24*

**Will God's plan work for me?** "So you have sorrow now, but I will see you again; then you will rejoice, and no one can rob you of that joy."

*John 16:22*

**How can I know God's plan worked for me?** "So when your faith remains strong through many trials, it will bring you much praise and glory and honor on the day when Jesus Christ is revealed to the whole world."

*I Peter 1:7b*

**Connecting with God's Word**

Have you accepted God's joy in your life?

**Responding to God's Word**

Is there anything you want to say to God?

**Celebrate**

What gift from God can you celebrate today?

# Day 6 - JOY

# God's Gift

**Joy changes how God sees us.** The Bible says God rejoices when we accept his way. Read *Luke 15:7.*

**Joy changes God's focus.** The Bible says God will grant us the joy of his presence. Read *Psalm 16:7-11.*

**Joy changes how we see ourselves.** We realize we are safe. God takes care of everything, including our enemies. Read *Psalm 63:6-11.*

**Joy changes our daily lives.** We see troubles as opportunities to build our endurance. Read *James 1:2-4.*

### Receiving God's Word

"Yet true godliness with contentment is itself great wealth. After all, we brought nothing with us when we came into the world, and we can't take anything with us when we leave it. So if we have enough food and clothing, let us be content."

*I Timothy 6:6-8*

### Connecting with God's Word

How do we live life joyfully?

### Responding to God's Word

Is there anything you want to say to God?

### Celebrate

What gift from God can you celebrate today?

# Day 7 - JOY
# To Share

Mary was merely looking forward to marrying Joseph when the angel Gabriel appeared. She learned the Lord was with her, and although she was a virgin, she would have a baby called the Son of God. She was afraid, but replied that she was God's servant and would willingly obey.

The young woman knew there'd be trouble ahead because of her obedience, but she didn't complain. Instead, she sang with joy. Luke recorded her song. "…How my spirit rejoices…for he took notice of me…" Read *Luke 1:26-56.*

Submitting to God changes our plans for the future to involve us in Kingdom work. However, devotion to him gives contentment as we come to understand that his plans for us are perfect. Like Mary, we may be afraid when he compels us to help, but joy comes knowing that our obedience allows God to look on us with favor.

Many people are restless and don't know why. Insecurity haunts them. They need the joy that comes knowing God will watch over them. If you have received the gift of joy, will you share?

## Receiving God's Word

"Mary responded, 'Oh, how my soul praises the Lord. How my spirit rejoices in God my Savior! For he took notice of his lowly servant girl, and from now on all generations will call me blessed. For the Mighty One is holy, and he has done great things for me. He shows mercy from generation to generation to all who fear him.'"

*Luke 1:46-50*

## Connecting with God's Word

What has God done for you?

## Responding to God's Word

Is there anything you want to say to God?

## Celebrate

What gift from God can you celebrate today?

*Melissa Kirk*

*Dear Lord,*

*Thank you for the privilege of asking you for anything. Thank you for the joy I have while trusting you to take care of my every need. Now I ask you to fill me with your love.*
*Amen*

*Melissa Kirk*

# LOVE

*Definition: willing to self-sacrifice*

"To love another person is to see the face of God."

Victor Hugo (Les Miserables)

# Day 1 - LOVE

## In Worship

**Proclamation**

**Love**

Love is a gift from God, *the Father*, made possible through Jesus, *God's Son*. I accept the gift through faith in the victory over death by Jesus, *my Savior*.

**How important is love?**

Love is my greatest expression in return for the love God has for me. He gave Jesus, who willingly sacrificed his life in my place.

**Where does love come from?**

God. Read *I John 4:7*.

**How much does God love me?**

He sent his Son to save me. Read *John 3:16-17*.

## Receiving God's Word

"If I could speak all the languages of earth and of angels, but didn't love others, I would only be a noisy gong or a clanging cymbal. If I had the gift of prophecy, and if I understood all of God's secret plans and possessed all knowledge, and if I had such faith that I could move mountains, but didn't love others, I would be nothing. If I gave everything I have to the poor and even sacrificed my body, I could boast about it; but if I didn't love others, I would have gained nothing."

*I Corinthians 13:1-3*

## Connecting with God's Word

According to the scripture, how important is love?

## Responding to God's Word

Is there anything you want to say to God about love?

## Celebrate

What gift from God can you celebrate today?

# Day 2 - LOVE

## The Past

Anna was also invited to the party. There were still plenty of gifts. To name a few:

· The elderly Jewish woman was close to God.

· Anna was a prophet.

· She lived safely in the temple.

· She got to see the baby Jesus.

· As a prophet, she was privileged to tell those who were waiting to be rescued that their salvation had come.

· Anna lived a long life.

Anna was only married seven years when her husband died. During her very long life, she could have grown bitter. Instead, she worshiped God day and night, trusting him to take care of all her needs.

Because she devoted her life to God, she was positioned to watch the promised Messiah in human flesh being presented to God at the temple. Read *Luke 2: 2, 36-38.*

Because she loved God wholeheartedly, she witnessed God's wholehearted love in action.

### Receiving God's Word

"Then she [Anna] lived as a widow to the age of eighty-four. She never left the Temple but stayed there day and night, worshiping God with fasting and prayer. She came along just as Simeon was talking with Mary and Joseph, and she began praising God. She talked about the child to everyone who had been waiting expectantly for God to rescue Jerusalem."

*Luke 2:37-38*

### Connecting with God's Word

How much do you love God?

### Responding to God's Word

Is there anything you want to say to God?

### Celebrate

What gift from God can you celebrate today?

# Day 3 - LOVE

# The Present

My parents divorced when I was two years old. Of course, I was too little to remember, but what I know is that I was probably the typical toddler, my sister was a preteen, and my brother was dying from cancer.

While sandwiched between one daughter's puberty and another's terrible twos, Mom dealt with hospitals, doctors, and her son's awful disease and ultimate death.

She worked hard to take care of the four of us. Money had to stretch and put food on the table. Babysitters had to be arranged.

I never remember doing without anything, though. But, I'm sure my mother did.

Jessie Marie did without calm – it was a period of uncertainness.

She did without luxuries. Without a car for many years, we walked to buy groceries and to the laundry mat.

She did without a social life – who had time?

She did without status. Many employers during her service years didn't offer equal pay for women. She learned that the hard way when her promised wage at a new job was reduced when the employer discovered "Jessie" was a female.

If something went wrong, she had to figure it out. If something broke, she fixed it.

My mother saved to be sure we had presents for Christmas. She saved so we had new clothes to start the school year. She passed up vacations, cashing in the extra pay for essentials.

She made sure we went to church. And school excursions.

I don't remember her ever taking a leisure trip without us. I don't remember her doing *anything* for herself.

What a living example of sacrificial love. I am forever blessed to have such a loving mother. While I was young, I never stopped to think about how much she gave up for the benefit of her children. Now, to say *thank you* is woefully inadequate, but other than trying to follow her example and unselfishly give, it's the best I can do.

Thank you, Mom.

As wonderful as she was, my mother had limits and made mistakes. She was human.

God has no limits. His love goes farther than any parents' ever could. He loves us all so much that he gave his only Son to cover our mistakes and bridge the gap our limits create. God, the Father, gave God, the Son. He gave himself for you and me!

My finite mind can't comprehend how unlimited God's love is. I don't have to understand it. I only have to trust him.

Thank you, God.

## Receiving God's Word

"For this is how God loved the world: He gave his one and only Son, so that everyone who believes in him will not perish but have eternal life."

*John 3:16*

## Connecting with God's Word

How much does God love you?

## Responding to God's Word

Is there anything you want to say to God?

## Celebrate

What gift from God can you celebrate today?

# Day 4 - LOVE

## The Future

The next breath we intend to take is the future. The Bible tells us what it should look like.

"Love is patient and kind. Love is not jealous or boastful or proud or rude. It does not demand its own way. It is not irritable, and it keeps no record of being wronged. It does not rejoice about injustice but rejoices whenever the truth wins out. Love never gives up, never loses faith, is always hopeful, and endures through every circumstance. Prophecy and speaking in unknown languages and special knowledge will become useless. But love will last forever!"

*I Corinthians 3:4-8*

God tells us the greatest thing that lasts forever is love. Read *I Corinthians 13:13*.

~A simple thought~
Life filled with love looks lovely.

**Receiving God's Word**

"This is my commandment: Love each other in the same way I have loved you. There is no greater love than to lay down one's life for one's friends. You are my friends if you do what I command."

*John 15:12-13*

**Connecting with God's Word**

How the scripture say we should love?

**Responding to God's Word**

Is there anything you want to say to God?

**Celebrate**

What gift from God can you celebrate today?

# Day 5 - LOVE

## God's Plan

### Receiving God's Word

**Do you need God's plan?** "We know how much God loves us, and we have put our trust in his love. God is love, and all who live in love live in God, and God lives in them."

*I John 4:16*

**Why do you need God's plan?** "But anyone who does not love does not know God, for God is love."

*I John 4:8*

**What is God's plan?** "For this is how God loved the world: He gave his one and only Son, so that everyone who believes in him will not perish but have eternal life."

*John 3:16*

**What is my part in God's plan?** "Jesus replied, 'you must love the LORD your God with all your heart, all your soul, and all your mind.' This is the first and greatest commandment. A second is equally important: 'Love your neighbor as yourself.'"

*Matthew 22:37-39*

**Will God's plan work for me?** "Can anything ever separate us from Christ's love? Does it mean he no longer loves us if we have trouble or calamity, or are persecuted, or hungry, or destitute, or in danger, or threatened with death? No, despite all these things, overwhelming victory is ours through Christ, who loved us."

*Romans 8:35, 37*

**How can I know God's plan worked for me?** "Such love has no fear, because perfect love expels all fear. If we are afraid, it is for fear of punishment, and this shows that we have not fully experienced his perfect love. We love each other because he loved us first."

*I John 4:18-19*

## Connecting with God's Word

Have you experienced God's love in your life?

## Responding to God's Word

Is there anything you want to say to God?

## Celebrate

What gift from God can you celebrate today?

# Day 6 - LOVE

## God's Gift

**Love changes how God sees us.** The Bible says he will never abandon the godly. Read *Psalm 37:28.*

**Love changes God's focus.** The Bible says God delights in his children. Read *Zephaniah 3:17.*

**Love changes how we see ourselves.** We are dead to ourselves and we trust Christ. Read *Galatians 2:20.*

**Love changes our daily lives.** We love our enemies and those who hurt us. Read *Luke 6:27.*

**Receiving God's Word**

"We know what real love is because Jesus gave up his life for us. So we also ought to give up our lives for our brothers and sisters. If someone has enough money to live well and sees a brother or sister in need but shows no compassion—how can God's love be in that person? Dear children, let's not merely say that we love each other; let us show the truth by our actions."

*I John 3:16-18*

**Connecting with God's Word**

What does the scripture say about God's gift of love?

**Responding to God's Word**

Is there anything you want to say to God?

**Celebrate**

What gift from God can you celebrate today?

# Day 7 - LOVE

## To Share

Imagine Joseph's shock when he found out Mary was pregnant. He knew it wasn't his child. Being a decent young man, he planned to break their engagement quietly to protect her.

But, an angel of the Lord appeared in his dreams and told him to go ahead and marry her. The conception of the baby was supernatural and the boy would be known as "God is with us."

The request probably disconcerted Joseph, but he obeyed. It was the first of many events that would require him to do the uncommon, and even risk his life to follow God's instructions. Read *Matthew 1:18-24, 2:1-23*.

Following God isn't always easy, but he has a big plan and is taking care of all the details.

As a Christ-Follower, you are part of his plan. He loves you and wants you to love others.

If you have received the gift of love, will you share?

### Receiving God's Word

"Joseph, her fiancé, was a good man and did not want to disgrace her publicly, so he decided to break the engagement quietly. As he considered this, an angel of the Lord appeared to him in a dream. 'Joseph, son of David,' the angel said, 'do not be afraid to take Mary as your wife. For the child within her was conceived by the Holy Spirit. And she will have a son, and you are to name him Jesus, for he will save his people from their sins.'"

*Matthew 1:19-21*

### Connecting with God's Word

How does the scripture demonstrate love?

### Responding to God's Word

Is there anything you want to say to God?

### Celebrate

What gift from God can you celebrate today?

*Dear Lord,*

*Thank you for loving me. Thank you for forgiving me. You alone are worthy of my praise. Help me as I share your love with others.*

*Amen*

*Melissa Kirk*

# The Gifts

## *Hope. Peace. Joy. Love.*

It's a blessing to be reminded of all that God has gifted us with. Whatever season of life you're in, I pray that you eagerly accept God's gifts. If you're having difficulties receiving them, just ask. God wants to have a conversation with you today.

The Bible says in John 1 that Jesus came to this earth as the light. God says the light will never be extinguished. Jesus died on the cross for everyone, paying the death penalty required because of sin. But, he defeated death and rose from the grave so you and I can have the opportunity for eternal life in a place called heaven, free from hurt and uncertainty.

We receive our inheritance when we believe God and accept Jesus as Lord. This is the greatest gift of all. If you haven't accepted it, I pray you will do so now. If you aren't sure how, everything you need to know is found on pages 16-17 – "Hope - God's Plan." I'd love to hear from you if you make this decision.

If you're reading this during the Advent season, make a point to be in the midst of the chaotic, commercialized, celebration. As a Christ-Follower, share your time, a broad smile, and a hug. Don't forget to tell others how important Christmas is. We return blessings to God when we commemorate the birth of our Savior and celebrate in anticipation his second coming to gather God's children.

*God sent his Son, Jesus. He is coming again, soon.*
*God sent a star to light our way. Celebrate and share hope.*
*God's heavenly hosts cried out. Celebrate and share peace.*
*God's gift is eternal life. Celebrate and share joy.*
*God's gift is available to all. Celebrate and share love.*
*God sent his Son, Jesus. He is coming again, soon.*

# READ MORE

*Melissa Kirk*

# GROUP DISCUSSION NOTES

For success, be sure to plan ahead. Invite participants to the study. Give them the book and assign the introduction and the first topic, "Hope" to be completed before the first meeting. Set up everything for each meeting before the starting time. Review the week's discussion and when possible, enlist volunteers in advance for scripture readings.

Keep the meeting short – an hour and one-half or less is plenty. Most important, keep it simple. A group time that discusses *ADVENT – Celebrate the Coming* should focus on God's gifts of hope, peace, joy, and love – not the commercialized chaos.

In advance: Prepare a sealed, wrapped gift box with a small slit in the top. This box will be used for participants to place private communications to God. Be sure to explain that the box is just symbolic because God can hear prayers anywhere. Always have small slips of paper and pens near the box.

Prepare a display. It should always include the

wrapped box and a white candle. Each week, add a candle representing the week of Advent being discussed. The following colored candles are recommended. Hope – purple. Peace – purple. Joy – pink. Love – purple. Another option is white candles with colored ribbons tied around them. By the end of the last week, all candles will be on display. You may also display all candles from week one. Just be sure to follow the weekly lighting instructions.

# **Optional** activities to include in your meetings:

› Refreshments. Decide if you will serve refreshments at the beginning or after the group discussion. Keep it consistent if possible.

› Have participants bring an item for the local food bank, nursing home, or children's home, etc. each week and assign someone to deliver the contributions after the final meeting.

› Ask volunteers in advance to do an activity. Examples are:

• Sing a Christmas Carol or lead the group in singing one.

• Read a Christmas poem.

· Watch a short YouTube video about the week's topic.

· Give a personal testimony.

· Lead a craft time that takes no more than fifteen minutes.

NOTE: Volunteers should have everything ready before the meeting begins so there won't be non-constructive down time. ALSO: Door prizes are always fun.

*Melissa Kirk*

# WEEK ONE – CELEBRATE HOPE

Welcome everyone and allow time for introductions if necessary.

1. Point to the display and say, "For the next four weeks, we will discuss the gifts God gave. This gift-wrapped box represents the gift of easy access to God; all because of Jesus. We can approach God anytime and anywhere about anything. Please feel free to use this box for any prayers or thoughts you want to share privately with God and symbolically release to his will and perfect plan. The contents of

the box will not be seen by anyone else."

As the leader, read *John 3:16*.

Open in prayer.

2. Hope – In Worship

    Light the candle representing hope.

    Responsive Reading: As a group, read aloud the first page of "In Worship" for the week of hope. The leader reads the words in bold letters followed by the group responding with the text. Enlist two participants to be prepared to read the included scriptures.

3. Any prearranged volunteer music, reading, or video would be appropriate now. Any craft activity time would be better after group discussion.

4. Hope – The Past

    Say "Zachariah was invited to a party and received gifts. What gift interested you the most and why?" Allow for discussion. Say "Have you ever doubted God would answer your prayer? Do you think you missed a blessing from God because of the doubt?" Allow for discussion.

5. Hope – The Present

   Say "Have you ever been in a dark period in your life? How did it feel to come out of that time?" Allow for discussion.

6. Hope – The Future

   Ask for a volunteer to read *Isaiah 9:2*.

   Say "Do you know someone who is going through a dark period in their life? What does it look like to you? Allow for discussion.

7. Hope – God's Plan

   Say "The scriptures listed together in this section are often called the Romans Road. Which scripture do you like the most?" Allow for discussion.

8. Hope – God's Gift

   Say "God offers hope through his Son, Jesus. How does it feel to accept hope?" Allow for discussion.

9. Hope – To Share

   Ask for a volunteer to read *I Peter 3:15*.

   Say "What does the Bible say about sharing hope?" Allow for discussion.

Say "Your assignment this week is to share hope with someone and study the topic of "Peace."

10. Prearranged volunteer crafts are appropriate here.

# WEEK TWO – CELEBRATE PEACE

Welcome everyone and allow time for introductions if necessary.

1. Point to the display and say, "I want to remind you that this box represents God's gift. It symbolizes our easy approach to him because of Jesus. Please feel free to use this box for any prayers or thoughts you want to share privately with God and symbolically release to his perfect will and plan. The contents of the box will not be seen by anyone

else."

As the leader, read *John 3:16*.

Open in prayer.

2. Peace – In Worship

   Light the candles representing hope and peace.

   Responsive Reading: As a group, read aloud the first page of "In Worship" for the week of peace. The leader reads the words in bold letters followed by the group responding with the text. Enlist two participants to be prepared to read the included scriptures.

3. Any prearranged volunteer music, reading, or video would be appropriate now. Any craft activity time would be better after group discussion.

4. Peace – The Past

   Say "Simeon was invited to the party and enjoyed it. What does it feel like to celebrate?" Discuss.

   Say "Has anyone received a blessing they would like to share with the group?" Allow for discussion.

5. Peace – The Present

Say "What does peace feel like to you?" Allow for discussion.

6. Peace – The Future

   Ask for a volunteer to read *Isaiah 40:31*.

   Say "Why is trust so important when it comes to having peace?" Allow for discussion.

7. Peace – God's Plan

   Say "What scripture about God's plan for peace stood out to you the most?" Allow for discussion.

8. Peace – God's Gift

   Say "What is the difference between being a friend of God versus being his enemy?" Allow for discussion.

9. Peace – To Share

   Ask for a volunteer to read *James 3:17-18*.

   Say "What does the Bible say about being a peacemaker?" Allow for discussion.

   Say "Your assignment this week is to share peace with someone and study the topic of "Joy.""

10. Prearranged volunteer crafts are appropriate here.

*Melissa Kirk*

# WEEK THREE – CELEBRATE JOY

Welcome everyone and allow time for introductions if necessary.

1.  Point to the display and say "I want to remind you that this box represents God's gift. It symbolizes our easy approach to him because of Jesus. Please feel free to use this box for any prayers or thoughts you want to share with God privately and symbolically release to his will and perfect plan. The contents of the box will not be seen by anyone else." As leader, read *John 3:16*.

Open in prayer.

2. Joy– In Worship

Light the candles representing hope, peace, and joy.

Responsive Reading: As a group, read aloud the first page of "In Worship" for the week of joy. The leader reads the words in bold letters followed by the group responding with the text. Enlist two participants to be prepared to read the included scriptures.

3. Any prearranged volunteer music, readings, or video would be appropriate now. Any craft activity time would be better after group discussion.

4. Joy – The Past

Say "Elizabeth was invited to the party and excitedly participated. What does it feel like to share your Christian faith with others?" Allow for discussion.

Say "Has anyone ever mentored you? Or, have you ever mentored anyone? What was the experience like?" Allow for discussion.

5.  Joy – The Present

    Say "What does joy feel like to you?" Allow for discussion.

6.  Joy – The Future

    Ask for a volunteer to read *Hebrew 12:1-2*. Say "Do you think a non-believer can have joy? Why or why not?" Allow for discussion.

7.  Joy – God's Plan

    Say "What scripture about God's plan for joy stood out to you the most?" Allow for discussion.

8.  Joy – God's Gift

    Say "How does God act toward a new Christ-Follower?" Allow for discussion.

9.  Joy– To Share

    Ask for a volunteer to read *Luke 1:46-50*.

    Say "What do you think Mary's greatest joy was?" Allow for discussion.

    Say "Your assignment this week is to share joy and study the topic "love" for next week."

10. Prearranged volunteer crafts are appropriate here.

*Melissa Kirk*

# WEEK FOUR – CELEBRATE LOVE

Welcome everyone and allow time for introductions if necessary.

1.  Point to the display and say, "I want to remind you that this box represents God's gift. It symbolizes our easy approach to him because of Jesus. Please feel free to use this box for any prayers or thoughts you want to share privately with God and symbolically release to his will and perfect plan. No one will see the contents."

    As the leader, read *John 3:16*. Open in prayer.

2.  Love – In Worship

    Light the candles representing hope, peace, joy and love. Responsive Reading: As a group, read aloud the first page of "In Worship" for the week of love. The leader reads the words in bold letters followed by the group responding with the text. Enlist two participants to be prepared to read the included scriptures.

3.  Any prearranged volunteer music, readings, or video would be appropriate at this time. However, any craft activity time would be better after group discussion.

4.  Love – The Past

    Say "Anna was invited to the party and devoted her whole life to God. Do you know someone who has devoted their entire life to God? What does/did it look like to you?" Allow for discussion.

5.  Love – The Present

    Say "Have you ever experienced sacrificial love?" Allow for discussion.

6.  Love – The Future

    Ask for a volunteer to read *I Corinthians 3:4-8*.

    Say "Jesus told the disciples that there was no

greater love than to lie down your life for a friend. How do you think he felt knowing he was going to do exactly that, and the disciples didn't understand?" Allow for discussion.

7. Love – God's Plan

Say "What scripture about God's plan for love stood out to you the most?" Allow for discussion.

8. Love – God's Gift

Say "What should our love for God look like?" Allow for discussion.

9. Love– To Share

Ask for a volunteer to read *Matthew 1:19-21*.

Say "What do you think Joseph's greatest sacrifice was when he obeyed and married Mary?" Discuss.

**Light the white candle.**

As a volunteer to read *John 1:6-14*.

Say "God showed us sacrificial love by sending Jesus into the world. The Bible says in John 1 that Jesus came to this earth as light for everyone. God says the light will never be extinguished. Jesus died on the cross, bearing the death penalty that had to be paid because of sin. He defeated death and rose from the grave so you and I can have the opportunity for eternal life in a place called heaven, free from death and decay. We receive that right and become children of God when we believe him and accept Jesus as Savior. It is the most important gift of all. His simple plan of *how* to accept the gift is on pages 16-17 of this book." Ask for a volunteer to read *Luke 2:6-16*.

Say "Advent is a time to commemorate the birth of Jesus, but it is also a special time to celebrate and anticipate Jesus' return to gather all God's children." Ask a volunteer to read *Revelation 22:1-6, 17*. Say "As Christ-Followers, we are called to love others as he loved us. God commissioned us to go out and be light for him. Your final assignment is to share that love with someone this week. Please repeat these words after me: **Amen! Come, Lord Jesus!**"

10. Prearranged volunteer crafts are appropriate here.

Excerpt

# GRACE WARRIOR
## *Bathed in Mercy, Clothed in Grace*
### Grace Warrior Devotional Series

*Melissa Kirk*

# Grace Warrior

If you are my sibling-in-Christ, then I know you've experienced the mercy of God. He met you at the cross. He stripped off the dirty, ugly, often tattered and worn-out life clothes, and as Psalm 103 says, he removed those rags as far as the east is from the west. At that moment, you became clean. And vulnerable.

I don't do clean well. By the end of the day, I will have evidence of everything I've eaten, and a lot of what I've said, all over me.

Vulnerable? When I find myself in unknown territory, I suddenly feel inadequate.

Mercy removed our guilt, but clean and vulnerable sounds hard, doesn't it? Well, we can thank God that he didn't stop with just mercy. What else happened at the cross?

Rest assured, we didn't catch the Almighty off guard.

God told the prophet, Jeremiah, that before he ever formed him in his mother's womb, he gave him an appointment.

Us too! God had a good and perfect will for each of us before we were ever born. What is your purpose? What is his plan for you?

You may not have it titled or thought much about it, but you know at least a little. You can probably think of times when you were poked or prodded in a different direction. Maybe you remember a time being squeezed or molded into a different thought pattern. Or perhaps, you've had a barrier thrown up on one of life's paths while an entire wall collapsed on another.

That's divine direction and holy intervention. God's plan for you is in full motion, and it's invading every part of your life.

What if, at the cross, God had said, "Welcome to the family! I've got a chore for you. Good luck with that." Huh?

He didn't. No, what God did when he bathed you in mercy, was to immediately clothe you in grace.

You are now dressed in the best. Those ugly and tattered rags are gone! Marvelous grace adorns you.

Do you know what the most amazing, priceless thing about your new *grace* clothes is? They will always fit you. Grace will dress you for every occasion in your life. Every situation!

God told Paul, "My grace is all you need. My power works best in weakness." Paul's weaknesses could have been physical ailments, or the authorities questioning his apostleship, or a combination of many things.

For you – whether your weakness is a limitation you've allowed yourself, or a constraint that someone else has placed on you, know that you are just like Paul. God has an endless supply of grace. Where you are weak, he is all powerful.

Friend, at the cross, he gave you mercy, purpose, and grace to fulfill that purpose.

He is the King. You are his child. He's given you a

task specifically designed for you; that only your shoes are meant to fill.

If you haven't experienced the mercy of God, this book will encourage and guide you to a better understanding of God's desire for you.

To my siblings-in-Christ, I hope you will consider what your purpose in God's plan is. Most important, I pray you will daily recognize God's grace and its potential through you.

God gave me mercy, purpose, and grace. Admittedly, I'm a work in progress. I'm Melissa Kirk, *grace warrior*. My task is to encourage you to rise with me as a warrior for the Kingdom, bathed in mercy, clothed in grace.

Excerpt

# GRACE WARRIOR
*At the King's Command*

Grace Warrior Devotional Series

*Melissa Kirk*

# The Edict

My mother loves the McIntosh variety apple. She says it's full of flavor, easy to digest, and bakes well. When they're in season, she loads up. I can be sure she will send some home with me because she knows I agree – they are delicious.

What makes it good is everything under its skin. The fruit thrives with a strong core, seed, flesh, and stem. Properly grown and harvested, it's pleasing to the taste buds. Just as God intended.

In similar fashion, everything good about us is under

our skin in impalpable life sources created by God; wholly designed to glorify him. As Christ-Followers, we are a sampling of his perfect flavor.

To enable us to yield the proper taste of his goodness, he issued an edict he calls the most important command.

"And you must love the Lord your God with all your heart, all your soul, all your mind, and all your strength."

*Mark 12:30*

This is a direct order between him and us which God doesn't trivialize. Our adoption into the kingdom came at the highest cost; the blood of Jesus. To say that he wants all our energy concentrated on all things godly would be wrong. He doesn't want it. He demands it.

The duty appears daunting, but here's the beautiful thing. He *created* our heart, soul, mind, and strength, and knows their full potential. If we yield to his authority, our human limitations cease to matter. God has high expectations and gives us his unlimited, all-powerful grace to overshadow our weaknesses.

We will never be able to fully embrace this command. The closest we come is if we willingly lay ourselves to be martyred. However, he knows we are imperfect people and is not only faithful to put our perceived failed attempts in right standing, but to also use them to bring attention to him.

What's under your skin? Does your heart beat for God? Does your soul reveal you prefer him over everything else? Is your mind calculating every move to benefit the Almighty? Are you using every ounce of your strength to follow his instruction?

It's our call to obedience. Friend, embrace it. God created you. He walks life's path with you. He preserves your life for the number of days he determines right. He's prepared an everlasting home for you. He loves you and has exciting plans for you. He watches over you as the apple of his eye.

Your next breath is dependent on him.

God adds a second command that he says is just as important.

"The second is equally important: 'Love your neighbor as yourself.' No other commandment is greater than these."

*Mark 12:31*

I believe obeying the second edict will subconsciously happen if we are complying with the first.

With this devotion, my prayer is that Christ-Followers will find the determination to follow God's command by reflecting on his Word.

If you aren't a Christ-Follower, I pray that you will come to an understanding of God's authority and your position with him.

# Thank you

Thank you to my fellow Christian Communicators: Lori Boruff, Mary Aucoin Kaarto, Andrea Merrell, Anne Elizabeth Denny, Lori Hudson, Sandra Lovelace, Elizabeth Brickman, Sharron K. Cosby, and Ellen E. Gee. Your testimonials are very dear to me. They communicate your personalities beautifully.

Thank you to the rest of my family and friends for your encouraging words.

And an extra special *thank you* to my husband, Larry, who ate bowl after bowl of cereal for supper, to allow me more time to write.

Thank you to my readers. I wish you the best God has to offer in all seasons of your life.

To follow my Grace Warrior blog, kindly visit www.MelissaKirk.ORG and subscribe to receive e-mail notifications. I promise not to flood your inboxes.

# Special Links

**Grace Warrior Blog**

www.MelissaKirk.ORG   or   www.TheGraceWarrior.com

**Facebook - Personal**

Melissa C Kirk

**Facebook – Author**

MelissaKirkAuthor

**Pinterest**

MelissaCKirk

**Twitter**

@melissackirk

**Google +**

Melissa C Kirk Grace Warrior

**Instagram**

https://www.instagram.com/melissackirk/

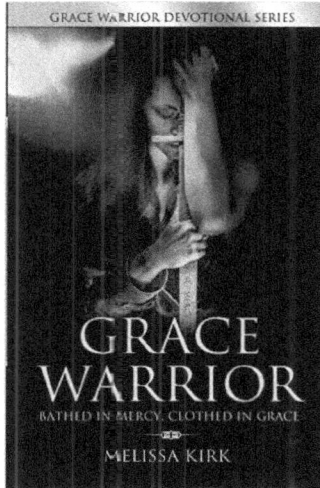

GRACE WARRIOR – *Bathed in Mercy, Clothed in Grace*

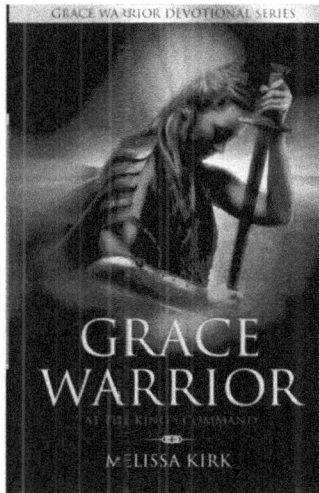

GRACE WARRIOR – *At the King's Command*

www.MelissaKirk.ORG   or   www.Amazon.com

Go in God's Grace

www.ingramcontent.com/pod-product-compliance
Lightning Source LLC
Chambersburg PA
CBHW020502030426
42337CB00011B/201